DISNEY LEARNING

DISNEY QUIZ MAGIC

DISNEY

THE LION KING

QUIZZES

HAKUNA ... ... MATATA

HEATHER E. SCHWARTZ

LERNER PUBLICATIONS ◆ MINNEAPOLIS

Mark your quiz answers on a separate sheet of paper.
Then check your answers when you're finished with the quiz!

Lerner Publications Company
A division of Lerner Publishing Group, Inc.
241 First Avenue North
Minneapolis, MN 55401 USA

For reading levels and more information, look up this title
at www.lernerbooks.com.

Main body text set in Avenir LT Pro 13/16 and ITC Lubalin Graph Std 12/15.
Typefaces provided by Linotype AG and International Typeface Corp.

Library of Congress Cataloging-in-Publication Data

Names: Schwartz, Heather E., author.
Title: The lion king quizzes : hakuna matata / Heather E. Schwartz.
Description: Minneapolis : Lerner Publications, 2019. | Series: Disney quiz
    magic | Includes bibliographical references.
Identifiers: LCCN 2018052798 (print) | LCCN 2018055347 (ebook) |
    ISBN 9781541561519 (eb pdf) | ISBN 9781541554733 (lb : alk. paper) |
    ISBN 9781541573970 (pb : alk. paper)
Subjects: LCSH: Lion king (Motion picture)—Miscellanea—Juvenile literature.
Classification: LCC PN1997.2.L557 (ebook) | LCC PN1997.2.L557 S39 2019
    (print) | DDC 791.43/72—dc23

LC record available at https://lccn.loc.gov/2018052798

Manufactured in the United States of America
1-45791-42673-1/22/2019

TABLE OF CONTENTS

THE WORLD OF THE LION KING

CAN YOU SING ALONG WITH ALL THE SONGS FROM *THE LION KING*? Do you wish you could live in the Pride Lands? Have you watched the movie again and again?

These quizzes will test your knowledge and help you get to know the characters better. See how you relate to the animals of the Pride Lands. Get ready to pick your own favorites and support your choices!

NOW IT'S TIME TO PROVE YOUR SUPERFAN STATUS!

WHICH *LION KING* SUPPORTING CHARACTER ARE YOU MOST LIKE?

1. Pick a snack.
- A. chocolate-covered crickets
- B. potato chips
- C. trail mix
- D. apple

2. Which game would you rather play?
- A. the floor is lava
- B. tickle fight
- C. dodgeball
- D. Red Light, Green Light

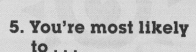

3. **After calling out the wrong answer in class, you . . .**
   A. raise your hand for the next question anyway
   B. make a joke
   C. give yourself credit for trying
   D. write down the correct answer

4. **How would you most like to travel?**
   A. hot-air balloon
   B. sailboat
   C. RV
   D. school bus

5. **You're most likely to . . .**
   A. run for class president
   B. play a prank on a rival team
   C. make a grumpy teacher laugh
   D. tutor classmates who need extra help

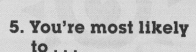

TURN THE PAGE FOR ANSWERS!

CHARACTER CONNECTION

Lion King characters are all brave in their own ways. Have you ever faced a situation that required courage?

YOU ARE MOST LIKE . . .

IF YOU ANSWERED MOSTLY As, you're like Shenzi. She's the leader of her group and always willing to take charge.

IF YOU ANSWERED MOSTLY Bs, you're like Timon. He jokes around and never fails to see the silly side of life.

IF YOU ANSWERED MOSTLY Cs, you're like Pumbaa. He's best known for his sense of humor but is also smart and caring.

IF YOU ANSWERED MOSTLY Ds, you're like Zazu. He is responsible, and his friends can count on him!

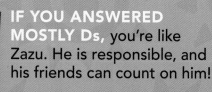

THE ROYAL FAMILY: TRUE OR FALSE?

1. RAFIKI IS SIMBA'S UNCLE.

2. SARABI IS THE QUEEN UNTIL SCAR TAKES THE THRONE.

3. AFTER MUFASA, THE THRONE RIGHTFULLY BELONGS TO SCAR.

4. ZAZU STOPS SERVING THE ROYAL FAMILY AFTER MUFASA IS KILLED.

5. NALA'S MOTHER IS SARABI.

COMPARE/CONTRAST

Simba and Scar both want to rule the Pride Lands but for different reasons. How do their reasons for wanting to rule show differences in their personalities?

1. False. Rafiki is not related to the royal family. 2. True. 3. False. The throne passes to the king's oldest child before it passes to the king's sibling. 4. False. He continues serving Scar and then Simba. 5. False. Nala's mother is Sarafina.

WHAT DO THESE WORDS FROM THE MOVIE MEAN?

1. *Hakuna matata* means . . .
   A. "Watch out."
   B. "No worries."
   C. "Be kind."

2. When Rafiki chants "Asante sana, squash banana," this is what he's saying in English:
   A. "Thank you, squash banana."
   B. "Squash banana, squash banana."
   C. "I love you, squash banana."

3. Simba's name is fitting because it means . . .

A. cub
B. lion
C. son

4. Pumbaa's name tells us he is . . .

A. always cheerful
B. sneaky
C. silly

5. Nala's name tells us she is . . .

A. a gift to the world
B. a female lion
C. a mother

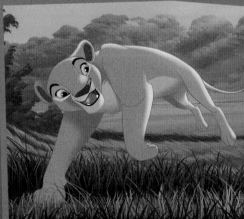

STORYTELLING SPOTLIGHT

The Lion King's creators used the African language Swahili in the movie. Some of the words and characters' names have Swahili meanings.

•WHAT KIND OF PRIDE LANDS LEADER WOULD YOU BE?

1. Choose a position in your favorite sport.
   A. scorekeeper
   B. coach
   C. team captain
   D. most improved player

2. Teachers would describe you as . . .
   A. quiet
   B. unique
   C. confident
   D. energetic

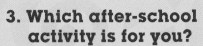

3. **Which after-school activity is for you?**
   A. chess club
   B. debate team
   C. student government
   D. ski club

4. **What role would you most like to have in a show?**
   A. director
   B. assistant director
   C. lead
   D. understudy

5. **Choose your ride.**
   A. tandem bike
   B. unicycle
   C. motorcycle
   D. hoverboard

TURN THE PAGE FOR ANSWERS!

COMPARE/CONTRAST

Mufasa and Simba are both leaders. How are their feelings about the Pride Lands the same? How are their actions as leaders different?

YOU'RE A LEADER LIKE . . .

IF YOU ANSWERED MOSTLY As, you're like Nala. You're a levelheaded leader who inspires others.

IF YOU ANSWERED MOSTLY Bs, you're like Rafiki. You know how to think outside the box, and people respect your ideas.

IF YOU ANSWERED MOSTLY Cs, you're like Mufasa. You're a leader whose inner strength shines through.

IF YOU ANSWERED MOSTLY Ds, you're like Simba. You bravely accept challenges and lead with a lively style.

WHO SANG IT: TRUE OR FALSE?

1. SCAR SINGS "I JUST CAN'T WAIT TO BE KING."

2. ZAZU SINGS "IT'S A SMALL WORLD" WHILE HE IS CAGED BY SCAR.

3. "BE PREPARED" IS MUFASA'S SONG TO SIMBA.

4. "HAKUNA MATATA" IS TIMON, PUMBAA, AND SHENZI'S MOTTO AND SONG.

5. SIMBA, NALA, TIMON, AND PUMBAA EACH SING DURING "CAN YOU FEEL THE LOVE TONIGHT?"

CHARACTER CONNECTION

Young Simba is so eager to be king that he says he can't wait. When have you wanted something you had to wait for? What did you do to make waiting easier?

1. False. Simba sings it. 2. True. 3. False. It is Scar's song about taking the throne. 4. False. Timon, Pumbaa, and Simba sing "Hakuna Matata." 5. True.

DO YOU KNOW YOUR WAY AROUND THE SAVANNA?

1. Who rules the Elephant Graveyard?
   A. Simba and Nala
   B. The hyenas
   C. Mufasa

2. Simba and Nala fall in love while running through . . .
   A. the Elephant Graveyard
   B. Hakuna Matata Falls
   C. the water hole

3. Simba can see all the land the light touches when he is standing on . . .
   A. Pride Rock
   B. Pumbaa's back
   C. Mount Everest

4. Rafiki draws a picture of Simba on . . .
   A. the Tree of Life
   B. Pride Rock
   C. the wall of a den

5. The wildebeest stampede takes place in . . .
   A. the Elephant Graveyard
   B. a dream
   C. the gorge

STORYTELLING SPOTLIGHT

The Elephant Graveyard is dark and shadowy to show it is a scary place. How do other settings show different moods throughout the story?

WHICH PRIDE LANDS ANIMAL WOULD YOU BE?

1. You'd most like to get to school . . .
   A. riding in a limo filled with your friends
   B. cruising around in a race car
   C. swinging on a zip line

2. Choose a school activity.
   A. acting in a play
   B. playing soccer
   C. reading in the library

3. You're the type of student who . . .
   A. likes working with others in group projects
   B. would rather be moving than sitting still
   C. is known for being quiet and thoughtful

4. The best thing about the internet is . . .
   A. sharing funny photos
   B. watching action-packed videos
   C. finding answers to your questions

5. It might be fun to try sleeping . . .
   A. under a shady tree
   B. standing up
   C. in a treehouse

TURN THE PAGE FOR ANSWERS!

COMPARE/CONTRAST

The animals in *The Lion King* have strong personalities. How do the animals behave like real-life animals?

YOU WOULD BE A . . .

IF YOU ANSWERED MOSTLY As, you would be a lion. Like the lions in Simba's pride, you enjoy doing things with others. You'd rather be in a group whenever you can.

IF YOU ANSWERED MOSTLY Bs, you would be a wildebeest. Like a wildebeest, you prefer being on the move. You are always looking for the next thing to do.

IF YOU ANSWERED MOSTLY Cs, you would be a mandrill like Rafiki. Like a mandrill, you can spend time with others but can also be alone. You enjoy adventure just as much as you like quiet time.

ALL ABOUT ZAZU: TRUE OR FALSE?

1. ZAZU ENJOYS GOING INTO THE HYENAS' BIRDIE BOILER.

2. MUFASA USES ZAZU TO HELP SIMBA WITH POUNCING PRACTICE.

3. ZAZU IS A PARROT.

4. ZAZU SERVES THE KING OF THE PRIDE LANDS.

5. ONLY THE KING CAN FIRE ZAZU.

CHARACTER CONNECTION

Zazu worries a lot, but it's only because he cares about others. What are ways you show your friends and family members that you care about them?

1. False. Zazu does not enjoy being shot out of a hot geyser. 2. True. 3. False. He is a red-billed hornbill. 4. True. 5. True.

CAN YOU FINISH THESE LINES FROM THE MOVIE?

1. Zazu tells Mufasa that Scar would make a good . . .
   - A. leader
   - B. throw rug
   - C. lawyer

2. When Simba asks "What's a motto?" Timon answers,
   - A. "It's a short phrase."
   - B. "It's a silly saying."
   - C. "Nothing! What's a motto with you?"

3. According to Pumbaa, home is where you rest your . . .

A. heart
B. hat
C. rump

4. Mufasa tells Simba a king's time as ruler rises and falls like . . .

A. the sun
B. the moon
C. a bouncing ball

5. When Simba, Nala, and Zazu escape the hyenas, Banzai says,

A. "Where did they go?"
B. "Hey, did we order this dinner to go?"
C. "I wasn't hungry anyway."

STORYTELLING SPOTLIGHT

Many *Lion King* characters have funny lines. How do their different types of humor tell you more about these characters?

HOW WOULD YOU HANDLE SCAR?

1. You're headed out for a hike with friends when it starts to rain. You . . .

   A. search the sky for sunshine
   B. search the closet for your raincoat
   C. suggest a new indoor plan for the day

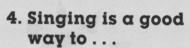

2. *The Lion King* characters you'd most like to spend time with are . . .

A. Timon and Pumbaa
B. Mufasa and the hyenas
C. the lionesses

3. When you're bored, you're most likely to . . .

A. invent a new game
B. call a friend
C. organize your things

4. Singing is a good way to . . .

A. show the world how happy you feel
B. make others happy
C. express thoughts and ideas

5. If you were a toy, you'd be . . .

A. a bouncy ball
B. a remote control helicopter
C. a modeling clay set

TURN THE PAGE FOR ANSWERS!

CHARACTER CONNECTION

Scar bullies others. What would you do if you saw someone bullying someone else? How would your actions help the person

YOU WOULD HANDLE SCAR AS . . .

IF YOU ANSWERED MOSTLY As, you would handle Scar as young Simba would. You see the sunny side of life and the best in others—even Scar!

IF YOU ANSWERED MOSTLY Bs, you would handle Scar as Zazu would. You find ways to defend yourself and take care of others too.

IF YOU ANSWERED MOSTLY Cs, you would handle Scar as Sarabi, Simba's mother, would. You're calm and sometimes quiet, but you speak up when it's needed.

•• SHENZI, BANZAI, AND ED: TRUE OR FALSE?

1. THE HYENAS FIRST SCARE SIMBA, NALA, AND ZAZU BY LAUGHING.

2. THE FIRST OF THE HYENAS TO SPEAK IN THE MOVIE IS BANZAI.

3. ED IS THE ONE TO POINT OUT THAT SIMBA AND NALA ARE ESCAPING.

4. SHENZI IS THE LEADER OF THE PACK.

5. THE HYENAS ARE ALL MALES.

COMPARE/CONTRAST

The hyenas in *The Lion King* are fierce like real hyenas. How are Shenzi, Banzai, and Ed different from hyenas you'd find in real life?

1. True. 2. False. The first to speak is Shenzi. 3. True. 4. True. 5. False. Banzai and Ed are males, and Shenzi is female.

MAKE YOUR OWN QUIZ!

WANT TO CREATE YOUR OWN *LION KING* QUIZ?
Copy the blank quiz on the next page. You could create a quiz to challenge your friends on how well they know the songs from the movie. Or create a quiz to guess where in the Pride Lands your friends would live.

MY

THE
LION KING
QUIZ:

COPY THIS PAGE!

_____

1. _____
   A. _____
   B. _____
   C. _____
   D. _____

2. _____
   A. _____
   B. _____
   C. _____
   D. _____

3. _____
   A. _____
   B. _____
   C. _____
   D. _____

FUN FACTS

A hidden Mickey Mouse head shows up during the song "I Just Can't Wait to be King." A monkey picks it off Zazu's head.

The wildebeest stampede is only six minutes long in the movie. However, it took about three years to animate.

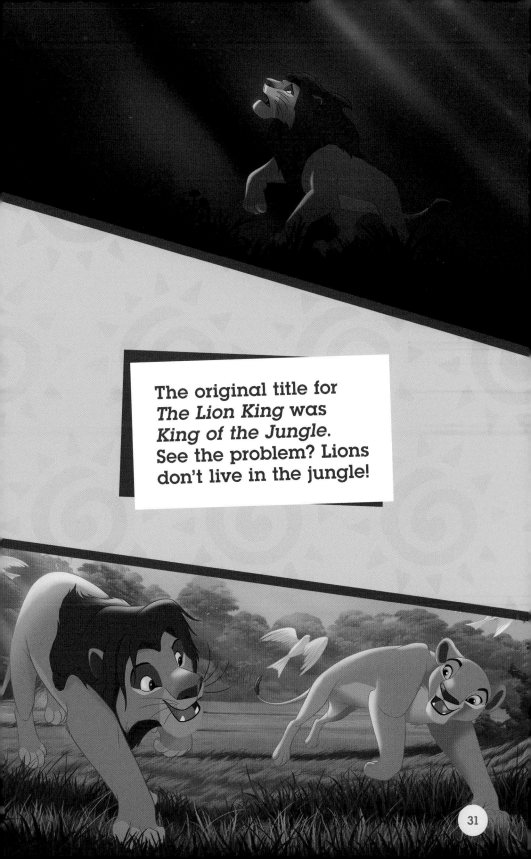

The original title for
The Lion King was
King of the Jungle.
See the problem? Lions
don't live in the jungle!

TO LEARN MORE

BOOKS

Olmanson, Shaina. *The Lion King Idea Lab*. Minneapolis: Lerner Publications, 2020.
Learn more about STEAM through these *Lion King* projects.

Schuh, Mari. *How to Be King of Pride Rock: Confidence with Simba*. Minneapolis: Lerner Publications, 2019.
Follow Simba's journey to building up the confidence he needs as the king of Pride Rock.

WEBSITES

Life Lessons from *The Lion King*
https://ohmy.disney.com/movies/2015/04/18/life-lessons-from-the-lion-king/
Visit this website to learn some life lessons from *The Lion King* movie.

The Lion King
https://movies.disney.com/the-lion-king
Watch scenes from the movie, download an activity pack, and more.